Mathematical structure

Unit guide

The School Mathematics Project

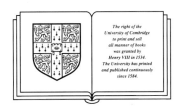

The right of the
University of Cambridge
to print and sell
all manner of books
was granted by
Henry VIII in 1534.
The University has printed
and published continuously
since 1584.

Cambridge University Press

Cambridge   New York   Port Chester   Melbourne   Sydney

Main authors   Chris Belsom
Stan Dolan
Paul Roder
Jeff Searle

Project director   Stan Dolan

The authors would like to give special thanks to Ann White for her help in preparing this book for publication.

Published by the Press Syndicate of the University of Cambridge
The Pitt Building, Trumpington Street, Cambridge CB2 1RP
40 West 20th Street, New York, NY 10011-4211, USA
10 Stamford Road, Oakleigh, Melbourne 3166, Australia

First published 1991

Produced by 16-19 Mathematics, Southampton

Printed in Great Britain by Scotprint Ltd., Musselburgh.

ISBN 0 521 42661 8

Contents

Introduction to the unit
(for the teacher)

This unit can be attempted before **any** other *16-19 Mathematics* unit. References to other A level work, such as elementary ideas of probability and the use of an example from *Problem solving*, can easily be made self-contained. *Mathematical structure* is therefore ideal as the first unit in a Further Mathematics course.

It is recognised that many students working through this unit may be doing so without the benefit of substantial contact time with a teacher. The unit has therefore been written to facilitate 'supported self-study'. It is assumed that even a minimal allocation of teacher time will allow contact at the start and end of each chapter and so

- solutions to all thinking points and exercises are in the students' text;

- a substantial discussion point in one of the opening sections enables the teacher to introduce each chapter;

- a special tutorial sheet can be used to focus discussion at a final tutorial on the work of the chapter.

Some of the ideas concerning binary operations will be met again in units such as *Matrices* and *Complex numbers*. The ideas of rigour and proof will be of value throughout the rest of the Further Mathematics course.

Chapter 1

By studying the underlying structure of a game, students should develop an appreciation of the importance of 'mathematical structure'. This opening chapter introduces the basic idea of a binary operation and important properties such as closure and associativity. These concepts form a common theme running through the unit.

Chapter 2

The discussion point for the first tutorial occurs in Section 2.2 but students should have no difficulty in reaching this point without teacher input. The discussion point deals with the issue of 'rigour'.

In this chapter, the value of pictorial methods for illustrating relationships is demonstrated whilst students should come to appreciate the power of formal algebraic methods in simplifying Boolean expressions and switching circuits. The last section on infinite sets and the related question on the tutorial sheet should stimulate discussion about both the history of mathematics and its continuing development.

Chapter 3

The idea of symmetry is used to introduce the important algebraic system known as a group. This topic provides an excellent example illustrating the ideas of binary operations introduced in the first chapter. In particular, structural ideas are very well illustrated by Lagrange's Theorem and the remarkable way that the structure of a subgroup helps to determine the structure of a containing group. The chapter also formalises ideas of isomorphism which were first met in the opening discussion point of Chapter 1.

Chapter 4

The final chapter considers a variety of methods of providing a convincing mathematical argument. The opening discussion point involves a problem which opens up a range of important ideas concerning proof and could be returned to later as as an application of mathematical induction.

As students work through other mathematics units they should be encouraged to increase the rigour of their arguments as their experience and competence increases. Their work on *Mathematical structure* should help them in this task.

Tasksheets

1 *Binary operations*

1.1   Structure

> **Play a number of games of 'fifteen-up'.**
> **Try to develop a strategy for playing the game.**

You may have decided upon strategies such as:

* choose 5 on the first go;

* if your opponent goes first and chooses 5, then choose an even number;

etc. Just as in 'noughts and crosses', there is a strategy which can never be beaten.

Whether or not you found an unbeatable strategy is not important. What is important is that you should have started to appreciate certain structural features of the game; features such as the fact that 5 is a special number (it is more likely than any other number to be in a set of 3 counters which add up to 15).

Any structural features you noticed will have helped you improve your strategy.

You may have felt that the game had certain similarities with 'noughts and crosses'. For example:

* there are nine possible choices;

* particular sets of 3 choices win;

* 5 is like the central square

and so on. In fact, the two games are essentially the same game! Choosing a particular number for 'fifteen-up' is equivalent to choosing the correspondingly numbered square in 'noughts and crosses'.

6	1	8
7	5	3
2	9	4

The two games therefore have precisely the same structure and any strategy for 'noughts and crosses' can be simply transformed into an equivalent strategy for 'fifteen-up'.

Tutorial sheet

1. (a)

$+_4$	0	1	2	3
0	0	1	2	3
1	1	2	3	0
2	2	3	0	1
3	3	0	1	2

(b)

$\times_{15}$	3	6	9	12
3	9	3	12	6
6	3	6	9	12
9	12	9	6	3
12	6	12	3	9

(c)

$\circ$	I	L	S	H
I	I	L	S	H
L	L	I	H	S
S	S	H	I	L
H	H	S	L	I

The table for $\times_{15}$ can be written

$\times_{15}$	6	3	9	12
6	6	3	9	12
3	3	9	12	6
9	9	12	6	3
12	12	6	3	9

which is clearly isomorphic to the table for (a), ($0 \leftrightarrow 6, 1 \leftrightarrow 3, 2 \leftrightarrow 9, 3 \leftrightarrow 12$).

The elements in (c) are all self-inverse which is not the case in (a) or (b) and so no other isomorphism can exist.

2. (a)

Cuboid

	I	X	Y	Z
I	I	X	Y	Z
X	X	I	Z	Y
Y	Y	Z	I	X
Z	Z	Y	X	I

Rectangle

	I	l	m	r
I	I	l	m	r
l	l	I	r	m
m	m	r	I	l
r	r	m	l	I

X, Y, Z are 180° rotations about the x, y, and z axes.

The isomorphism with the combination table for a rectangle is
$$X \leftrightarrow l, \quad Y \leftrightarrow m, \quad Z \leftrightarrow r$$

(continued)

(b) Let the reflections in $x = 0$, $y = 0$, $z = 0$ be denoted by x, y, z respectively.

Then $xy = Z$, $xz = Y$, $xx = I$
      $yx = Z$, $yz = X$, $yy = I$
      $zx = Y$, $zy = X$, $zz = I$

	I	X	Y	Z	x	y	z
I	I	X	Y	Z	x	y	z
X	X	I	Z	Y	?	z	y
Y	Y	Z	I	X	z	?	x
Z	Z	Y	X	I	y	x	?
x	x	?	z	y	I	Z	Y
y	y	z	?	x	Z	I	X
z	z	y	x	?	Y	X	I

[Having a labelled box is very useful for completing the table.]

The result of each of **Xx, Yy, Zz, xX, yY** and **zZ** is not a member of the elements defined so far.

The result of all of these is to move each corner of the box to the diagonally opposite corner - a central inversion.

(c) Calling the central inversion **C**, the complete table is

	I	X	Y	Z	x	y	z	C
I	I	X	Y	Z	x	y	z	C
X	X	I	Z	Y	C	z	y	x
Y	Y	Z	I	X	z	C	x	y
Z	Z	Y	X	I	y	x	C	z
x	x	C	z	y	I	Z	Y	X
y	y	z	C	x	Z	I	X	Y
z	z	y	x	C	Y	X	I	Z
C	C	x	y	z	X	Y	Z	I

2. Set algebra

2.2   Boolean algebra

> **Which of the following are identities?**
>
> (a) $(A \cup B)' = A' \cap B'$ (b) $(A \cap B)' = A' \cap B'$
>
> (c) $(A \cap B)' = A' \cup B'$ (d) $(A \cup B)' = A' \cup B'$
>
> **How would you convince someone that you are right ?**

Venn diagrams showing the regions are

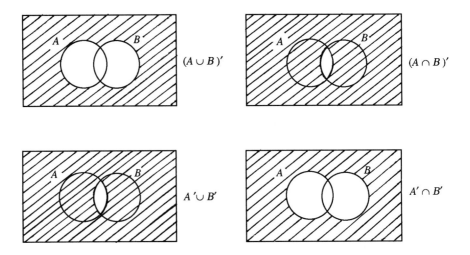

The diagrams show that $(A \cup B)' = A' \cap B'$ and $(A \cap B)' = A' \cup B'$ so (a) and (c) are identities.

The Venn diagram method of showing identities depends upon the diagram covering all possible cases. For example, a Venn diagram which shows the sets A and B as disjoint could not be used as a basis for a convincing argument. Mathematicians do not consider a pictorial approach using Venn diagrams to be sufficiently rigorous.

A more rigorous proof hinges on the fact that the equality of two sets, P and Q, is demonstrated if it can be proved that

$$P \subseteq Q \qquad (P \text{ is a subset of } Q)$$

$$\text{and} \quad Q \subseteq P \qquad (Q \text{ is a subset of } P)$$

12

Hence the identity $(A \cup B)' = A' \cap B'$ can be established by proving that

$$(A \cup B)' \subseteq A' \cap B' \quad \text{and} \quad A' \cap B' \subseteq (A \cup B)'$$

For example:

$$x \in (A \cup B)' \quad \Rightarrow \quad x \notin A \cup B$$
$$\Rightarrow \quad x \notin A \quad \text{and} \quad x \notin B$$
$$\Rightarrow \quad x \in A' \quad \text{and} \quad x \in B'$$
$$\Rightarrow \quad x \in A' \cap B',$$

Therefore $\qquad\qquad (A \cup B)' \subseteq A' \cap B'.$

$$x \in A' \cap B' \quad \Rightarrow \quad x \in A' \text{ and } x \in B'$$
$$\Rightarrow \quad x \notin A \quad \text{and } x \notin B$$
$$\Rightarrow \quad x \notin A \cup B$$
$$\Rightarrow \quad x \in (A \cup B)'$$

Therefore $\qquad\qquad A' \cap B' \subseteq (A \cup B)'$

$(A \cup B)'$ and $A' \cap B'$ are therefore equal and the identity (a) is proved. Similarly, (c) can be proved to be an identity.

The fact that (b) and (d) are not identities can be seen easily from the diagram. The easiest way to convince anyone is to give a counterexample.

The same counterexample can be used for both (b) and (d):

$$\varepsilon = \{1\}, \quad A = \{1\}, \quad B = \varnothing$$

Tutorial sheet

1. (a) The circuit can be represented more simply as

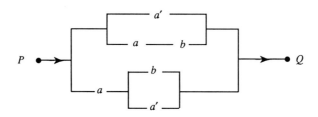

The Boolean expression is

$$(a' \cup (a \cap b)) \cup (a \cap (a' \cup b))$$

(b) The expression can be simplified as follows:

	$((a' \cup a) \cap (a' \cup b)) \cup ((a \cap a') \cup (a \cap b))$	*distributive law*
$=$	$(\varepsilon \cap (a' \cup b)) \cup (\varnothing \cup (a \cap b))$	*complement laws*
$=$	$(a' \cup b) \cup (a \cap b)$	*identity laws*
$=$	$a' \cup (b \cup (a \cap b))$	*associative law*
$=$	$a' \cup (b \cup (b \cap a))$	*commutative law*
$=$	$a' \cup b$	*absorption law*

(c)

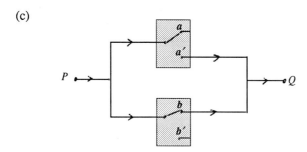

2. The diagram shows a one-to-one correspondence between all the points on the line and the points on the semi-circle (excluding its end points). Both intervals (and any other interval of non-zero length) have cardinality the infinity of the continuum.

3 *Group theory*

3.2   Transformations

> **Starting from a blank 4 x 5 board, can you form pattern A?**
>
> **Starting from a blank *m* x *n* board, what patterns can be formed?**
>
> **Justify your answers.**

While trying to answer these questions you should have tried plenty of practical experimentation with patterns on 4 x 5 and other sized boards.

You may have discovered experimentally that, for any size of board, the only patterns which could be formed are ones where each column is the same as the first column or its 'opposite'. (A similar result holds for rows.) You **cannot** therefore transform a blank board into pattern A.

To prove that this **must** always hold you could argue as follows:

The combination of flips is commutative and so **any** sequence of flips can be simplified into a series of row flips followed by a series of column flips. After the row flips all the columns are the same and then the column flips simply reverse some columns.

One way of analysing problems connected with the scoreboard is to consider the **group of transformations** generated by the row and column flips, R_i and C_j. The ideas given below depend upon the theory developed in this chapter and could be returned to during or after your work on group theory.

- The combination of the flips is both commutative and associative and so any series of flips can be simplified into a series of row flips followed by a series of column flips. Furthermore, the flips can be put into numerical order, for example:

$$C_2 C_1 R_1 C_2 R_3 = C_2 C_2 C_1 R_3 R_1$$
$$= C_1 R_3 R_1.$$

- All elements of the group are self inverse and so two sequences of flips are the same only if their combined effect is the identity transformation.

This is of relevance to the thinking point. Since

$$C_5 C_3 C_2 R_3 R_1 = C_4 C_1 R_4 R_2 \text{ because}$$
$$(C_5 C_3 C_2 R_3 R_1)(C_4 C_1 R_4 R_2) = C_5 C_4 C_3 C_2 C_1 \ R_4 R_3 R_2 R_1$$
$$= \mathbf{I}, \text{ the identity transformation.}$$

Group tables

1.　(i)　and (ii) are closed.

　　(iii)　**I** is a new element, so the table is not closed.

2.　(a)　The row and column corresponding to **I** are the same as the row and column, respectively, outside the body of the table.

　　(b)　(i)　No identity:　$ac = a$　and　$bc = b$　but　$ca \neq a$　and　$cb \neq b$

　　　　(ii)　No identity:　$ab = b$　and　$ac = c$　but　$ba \neq b$　and　$ca \neq c$

　　　　(iii)　b is an identity.

3.　(a)　$R\,R^2 = R^2\,R = I$　　　　**R** and R^2 are inverses of each other.
$$\left.\begin{array}{l} L\,L = I \\ M\,M = I \\ N\,N = I \end{array}\right\}$$　　**L, M, N** are 'self-inverse'.

　　(b)　In table (iii), b is the identity　and　$ac = ca = b$.　So a and c are inverses of each other.

　　　　Tables (i) and (ii) have no identity, so cannot include pairs of inverse elements.

　　(c)　A reflection.

Cyclic groups

1.

	I	R	R²
I	I	R	R²
R	R	R²	I
R²	R²	I	R

2.

square

	I	R	R²	R³
I	I	R	R²	R³
R	R	R²	R³	I
R²	R²	R³	I	R
R³	R³	I	R	R²

pentagon

	I	R	R²	R³	R⁴
I	I	R	R²	R³	R⁴
R	R	R²	R³	R⁴	I
R²	R²	R³	R⁴	I	R
R³	R³	R⁴	I	R	R²
R⁴	R⁴	I	R	R²	R³

hexagon

	I	R	R²	R³	R⁴	R⁵
I	I	R	R²	R³	R⁴	R⁵
R	R	R²	R³	R⁴	R⁵	I
R²	R²	R³	R⁴	R⁵	I	R
R³	R³	R⁴	R⁵	I	R	R²
R⁴	R⁴	R⁵	I	R	R²	R³
R⁵	R⁵	I	R	R²	R³	R⁴

Each row and column is a repeat of the previous one, with each element shifted one left or one up respectively.

3.

	2	1	3	0
2	0	3	1	2
1	3	2	0	1
3	1	0	2	3
0	2	1	3	0

This is still the table of a cyclic group. The 'cyclic property' can only be seen easily for some orderings of the group elements.

4.   (a)   There is an isomorphism between the elements of the group of rotations of a square and $\mathbb{Z}_4$, as can be seen in the combination tables.

square

	I	R	R²	R³
I	I	R	R²	R³
R	R	R²	R³	I
R²	R²	R³	I	R
R³	R³	I	R	R²

isomorphism

$I \leftrightarrow 0$

$R \leftrightarrow 1$

$R^2 \leftrightarrow 2$

$R^3 \leftrightarrow 3$

$\mathbb{Z}_4$

	0	1	2	3
0	0	1	2	3
1	1	2	3	0
2	2	3	0	1
3	3	0	1	2

  (b)   I and R² are self-inverse   0 and 2 are self-inverse

(continued)

5. (a) is a cyclic group.

     The table can be rearranged as

	d	b	a	c
d	d	b	a	c
b	b	a	c	d
a	a	c	d	b
c	c	d	b	a

    (b) is not a cyclic group because all the elements are self-inverse,

    (c) is not a group (of any sort) because there is no identity.

6.

$\times_8$	1	3	5	7
1	1	3	5	7
3	3	1	7	5
5	5	7	1	3
7	7	5	3	1

    This is not cyclic because **all** the elements are self-inverse.

Cayley's theorem

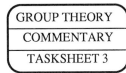
1.   (a) r^2 rotates the positions so that 1 moves to 3's position, 3 moves to 2's position and 2 moves to 1's previous position.

       (b) rs swaps the positions of objects 2 and 3.

       (c) sr^2 swaps the positions of objects 2 and 3.

2.   (a), (b) and (c) are the same.
         (d), (e) and (f) are the same.

3.   ① $s \circ s = e$ can be used to simplify any expressions with two s's together.

$$\text{e.g. } s \circ s \circ r = (s \circ s) \circ r = r.$$

       ② $r \circ r \circ r = e$ can be used to simplify any expression with three r's together.

$$\text{e.g. } s \circ r \circ r \circ r \circ s = s \circ (r \circ r \circ r) \circ s$$
$$= s \circ s$$
$$= e$$

       ③   To bring about a situation where rules ① and ② can be used, any s can be moved left by using $r \circ s = s \circ r \circ r$.

$$\text{e.g. } s \circ r \circ s = s \circ (s \circ r \circ r)$$
$$= (s \circ s) \circ r \circ r$$
$$= r \circ r$$

In this way all expressions can be simplified to ones where all s's are to the left of all r's and where there is at most one s and at most two r's i.e. $\{e,\ r,\ r^2,\ s,\ sr,\ sr^2\}$.

4.   (a)   There are six possible permutations as given in the table on Tasksheet 3.

	Permutation
1 2 3 → 1 2 3	e
1 2 3 → 1 3 2	sr^2
1 2 3 → 2 1 3	s
1 2 3 → 2 3 1	r^2
1 2 3 → 3 1 2	r
1 2 3 → 3 2 1	sr

One permutation followed by another is still a permutation of the objects and so the set of permutations is closed. The identity is e, r and r^2 are inverses of each other and all other elements are self inverse. Associativity holds for combinations of **all** transformations, because, for transformations, $a \circ (b \circ c)$ and $(a \circ b) \circ c$ both mean c followed by b followed by a.

(continued)

(b) The fact that each permutation can be expressed as combinations of r and s is shown in the table.

(c) r alone generates expressions of the form $r, r \circ r, r \circ r \circ r, r \circ r \circ r \circ r$, etc. Since $r \circ r \circ r = e$, this sequence only consists of the elements e, r and r^2.

Similarly, $s \circ s = e$ can be used to simplify any combination of s's into e or s.

5. (a) Object $\boxed{1}$ can move to one of 4 positions. For each of these, object $\boxed{2}$ can move to one of the remaining 3 positions. Then $\boxed{3}$ can move to one of the 2 positions left and $\boxed{4}$ then has only 1 possible position.

There are therefore $4 \times 3 \times 2 \times 1$ permutations.

(b) The same reasoning as in (a) applied to n objects gives

$$n \times (n-1) \times \dots \times 1 = n! \text{ permutations.}$$

(c) For the symmetries of a square, $\boxed{1}$ can move to one of 4 positions. For each of these, $\boxed{2}$ can move to one of the 2 adjoining positions. The positions of $\boxed{3}$ and $\boxed{4}$ are then determined.

There are therefore 4×2 symmetries.

6.

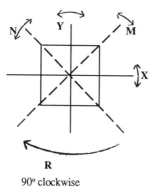

R
90° clockwise

The symmetries are

• The identity transformation, **I.**

• Reflections **M, N, X, Y.**

• Rotations **R, R²** and **R³.**

Subgroups generated by single elements are:

{I}
{I, M}, {I, N}, {I, X}, {I, Y}, {I, R²},
{I, R, R², R³}

Those generated by two elements are

{I, M, N, R²}, {I, X, Y, R²} and the whole group. (The whole group is generated, for example, by **X** and **R**.)

(continued)

Group tables revisited

1.

	I	R²	R	L	N	M
I	I	R²	R	L	N	M
R²	R²	R	I	N	M	L
R	R	I	R²	M	L	N

2.

	I	L	R	N	R²	M
I	I	L	R	N	R²	M
L	L	I	N	R	M	R²

3.

	I	M	R	L	R²	N
I	I	M	R	L	R²	N
M	M	I	L	R	N	R²

	I	N	R	M	R²	L
I	I	N	R	M	R²	L
N	N	I	M	R	L	R²

4 and 5.

	I	R	R²	R³	A	L	B	M
I	I	R	R²	R³	A	L	B	M
R	R	R²	R³	I	L	B	M	A
R²	R²	R³	I	R	B	M	A	L
R³	R³	I	R	R²	M	A	L	B
A	A	M	B	L	I	R³	R²	R
L	L	A	M	B	R	I	R³	R²
B	B	L	A	M	R²	R	I	R³
M	M	B	L	A	R³	R²	R	I

6.

	I	L	M	R²	R	A	B	R³
I	I	L	M	R²	R	A	B	R³
L	L	I	R²	M	A	R	R³	B
M	M	R²	I	L	B	R³	R	A
R²	R²	M	L	I	R³	B	A	R

7. For any subgroup you choose, the other elements can be arranged to show the 'repeated pattern' idea.

	I	R²	A	B	L	M	R	R³
I	I	R²	A	B	L	M	R	R³
R²	R²	I	B	A	M	L	R³	R

The only possible subgroups have either 1, 2, 4 or 8 elements. (The 1-element subgroup is simply {I}, the 8-element one is the entire group.)

Fermat's Little Theorem

1.   (a)   The remainders are 0, 1, 2, 3, 4, 5, 6 respectively

      (b)   The pattern 0, 1, 2, 3, 4, 5, 6 is repeated over and over again.

             If you multiply out

             $$(7 + a)^7 = (7 + a)(7 + a) \ \ ... \ \ (7 + a)$$

             then every term has a factor of 7 apart (possibly) for a^7. So $(7 + a)^7$ and a^7 have the same remainder when divided by 7. The 0, 1, 2, 3, 4, 5, 6 pattern is therefore repeated without limit.

2.   Since $\{1, 2, 3, 4, 5, 6\}$ is a group of order 6, the order of each element is 1, 2, 3 or 6 by Lagrange's Theorem. In particular, $a^6 = 1$ for every element a, since 1 is the identity.

      For $a \in \{1, 2, 3, 4, 5, 6\}$, $a^6 \equiv 1$ (modulo 7)

      $$\Rightarrow a^7 = a \cdot a^6 \equiv a \ (\text{modulo } 7)$$

3.   The result holds for any prime number.

4.   All terms of $(p + a)^p$ have a factor of p except (possibly) a^p. Then
      $$(p + a)^p - (p + a) \equiv a^p - a \ (\text{modulo } p).$$
      It is therefore only necessary to consider 0, 1, ..., $p - 1$.

5. $a^n \equiv 1$ (modulo p), because 1 is the identity of the group.

      The elements generated by a form a subgroup of order n. Therefore n divides $p - 1$, by Lagrange's theorem.

      In particular, $a^{p-1} \equiv 1$ (modulo p).

      Now $a^p - a = a\,(a^{p-1} - 1)$ and either $a \equiv 0$ (modulo p) or $a^{p-1} - 1 \equiv 0$ (modulo p). Hence p divides $a^p - a$.

Groups with 6 elements

1. The order of the group is 6.

   The order of any element must divide 6 and so is 1, 2, 3 or 6. The group is non-cyclic and so has no element of order 6. Thus $a^2 = e$ or $a^3 = e$. (If $a = e$ then $a^2 = e$.)

2. If every element satisfies $a^2 = e$ then every element is self-inverse.

   Let a be one element of order 2, then the elements can be arranged so that the pattern $\begin{array}{cc} e & a \\ a & e \end{array}$ is repeated along the top two rows.

3. Every element is self-inverse and so the elements a, b and ab are self-inverse i.e.

   $$(ab)\,(ab) = e \quad \text{and} \quad (aa)\,(bb) = e$$

   $\Rightarrow \quad (ab)\,(ab) = (aa)\,(bb)$

   $\Rightarrow \quad a\,(ba)\,b = a\,(ab)\,b \qquad$ Associativity

   $\Rightarrow \qquad\qquad ba = ab \qquad$ Cancellation

   $\Rightarrow \qquad\qquad ba = c.$

4. Since $f^3 \neq e$, you know from question 1 that $f^2 = e$. Similarly, $g^2 = h^2 = e$.

5.
   $g = af$

   $\Rightarrow gf = (af)f$

   $\quad\;\; = a\,(ff)$

   $\quad\;\; = ae$

   $\quad\;\; = a$

   Then $a = gf$

   $\Rightarrow ga = g\,(gf)$

   $\quad\;\; = (gg)\,f$

   $\quad\;\; = ef$

   $\quad\;\; = f.$

   The table can now be completed by using the Latin square property:

	e	a	a^2	f	g	h
e	e	a	a^2	f	g	h
a	a	a^2	e	g	h	f
a^2	a^2	e	a	h	f	g
f	f	h	g	e	a^2	a
g	g	f	h	a	e	a^2
h	h	g	f	a^2	a	e

   This is isomorphic to the symmetry group of an equilateral triangle given on Tasksheet 4:

   $e \leftrightarrow \mathbf{I}, \quad a \leftrightarrow \mathbf{R} \quad a^2 \leftrightarrow \mathbf{R^2} \quad f \leftrightarrow \mathbf{L} \quad g \leftrightarrow \mathbf{M} \quad h \leftrightarrow \mathbf{N}.$

Tutorial sheet

1.

	I	R	M	N
I	I	R	M	N
R	R	I	N	M
M	M	N	I	R
N	N	M	R	I

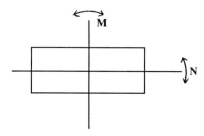

R - rotation $180°$

    (a)   **I** generates {**I**}
              R generates {**I, R**}, because $\mathbf{R}^2 = \mathbf{I}$
              M generates {**I, M**}
              N generates {**I, N**}

    (b)   No element generates the whole group and so it is **not** cyclic.

2. $\mathbb{Z}_8$

For example, {0, 1, 2, 3, 4, 5, 6, 7} under addition modulo 8 has the subgroup {0, 2, 4, 6}.

In fact, a cyclic group of order n has **precisely** one subgroup of each order which divides n.

3.

	I	C_1	C_2	R
I	I	C_1	C_2	R
C_1	C_1	I	R	C_2
C_2	C_2	R	I	C_1
R	R	C_2	C_1	I

This group is isomorphic to K.

4. $ef = f$ (e is identity)
      Also, $ef = e$ (f is identity)
          $\Rightarrow e = f$ as required.

Each group has **precisely** one identity element.

(continued)

5.　　(a)

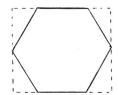

There are three such rectangles, each giving rise to a different subgroup isomorphic to K.

(b)　　There are two such triangles, but these give rise to the **same** subgroup, the one containing all the reflections in the lines joining mid-points of opposite edges.

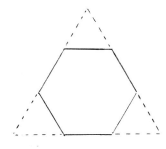

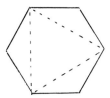

The other subgroup isomorphic to S_3, the one containing all the reflections in lines joining opposite points of the hexagon, arises from either of the two triangles like the one shown alongside.

6.　　The subgroup generated by r and s contains further subgroups $\{e, r, r^2\}$ and $\{e, s\}$. By Lagrange's theorem, its order is therefore divisible by 6.

In fact it contains precisely six elements e, r, r^2, s, rs, r^2s as can be seen from drawing up a combination table. The completed table is closed as shown below.

	e	r	r^2	s	rs	r^2s
e	e	r	r^2	s	rs	r^2s
r	r	r^2	e	rs	r^2s	s
r^2	r^2	e	r	r^2s	s	rs
s	s	r^2s	rs	e	r^2	r
rs	rs	s	r^2s	r	e	r^2
r^2s	r^2s	rs	s	r^2	r	e

The subgroup is isomorphic to S_3.

4 *Mathematical proof*

4.1 Introduction

1.   (a) **How can they get across?**

         (b) **What is the least number of trips needed to get them across?**

         (c) **How would you convince someone of your result for (b)?**

2.   **Generalise your method for *m* adults and *n* children and**

         (a) **find an algorithm for performing the transfer;**

         (b) **show that your algorithm works;**

         (c) **find the least possible number of trips;**

         (d) **justify your result for (c).**

This discussion point, if considered thoroughly, can be used to explore various aspects of mathematical proof. A first 'solution' of the problem is obtained by playing around with various possibilities. This exploratory work raises other issues which can be 'solved' in the particular instance and then proved more generally.

1.   (a)   It soon becomes clear that 2 children must cross first so that one of them can bring the boat back. An adult can then row across; the boat being brought back by the remaining child. The net effect is that one adult has been moved to the other bank. Repeating this procedure will transfer the other adult. The children are then transferred by two crossing, one returning and, finally, two crossing.

      (b)   For each adult the trips are:

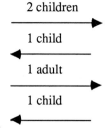

          4 journeys are needed per adult and so transferring both adults requires 8 trips.

There are then 3 further trips

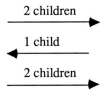

2 children

1 child

2 children

and so the total number of trips is 11.

(c)   The argument above would probably convince most people! A more formal proof is given in the answer to 2(d).

2.   (a)   Providing the number of children is at least 2, the process discussed in 1(b) provides the basic algorithm.

- Repeat the process

    2 children row across
    1 child rows back
    1 adult rows across
    1 child rows back

until no adult remains to be transferred.

- Then repeat the process

    2 children row across
    1 child rows back

until the number of children needing to be transferred is precisely 2.

- A final trip completes the transfer:

    2 children row across

You could try drawing a flow diagram for this procedure. You might include an analysis of the cases $n = 0$ and $n = 1$.

(b)   Proving the correctness of algorithms is an increasingly important mathematical topic. Essentially it involves carefully checking what the algorithm does for **all** possible inputs.

It is often necessary to both check some particular cases **and** show that the algorithm reduces all other cases to ones you have already checked.

For the river crossing, an important part of the check would be to convince yourself that the procedure successfuly reduces the number of adults needing transfer to zero. A rigorous proof of this requires the technique of mathematical induction developed in section 4.5. If you had considered values of n less than 2 then a large number of special cases would need to be considered e.g.

$n = 0, \ m = 0$

$n = 0, \ m = 1$

$n = 0, \ m \geq 2$ (In this case the crossing is impossible.)

$n = 1, \ m = 0$

$n = 1, \ m \geq 1$

etc.

This form of exhaustive analysis is considered in section 4.2.

(c)   If $n \geq 2$, the algorithm in (a) results in

$$
\begin{array}{ll}
4m \ \text{trips} & \text{(for } m \text{ adults)} \\
+ \ 2(n - 2) \ \text{trips} & \text{(to transer all but 2 children)} \\
+ \quad 1 \quad \text{trip} & \text{(for the last 2 children)}
\end{array}
$$

The total is therefore $4m + 2n - 3$.

(d)   A mathematical proof requires an argument which convinces you of the correctness of the result. The following argument should remove any doubt you might have about there possibly being a 'better' way to transfer the people than the one already given.

For any position, assign the score

2 x No. of adults on far bank + No. of children on far bank

Each crossing increases the score by at most 2.
Each return crossing decreases the score by at least 1.

A completed transfer consisting of, say, $k + 1$ crossings and k return crossings therefore increases the score by at most $2(k + 1) - k = k + 2$.

So $k + 2 \geq 2m + n$

$\Rightarrow$ $k \ \geq 2m + n - 2$

$\Rightarrow$ $2k + 1 \geq 4m + 2n - 3$

The least possible number of trips is $4m + 2n - 3$.

Some proofs using contradiction

1. $138 = 2 \times 69$ or $138 = 3 \times 46$
    $\quad\; = 2 \times 3 \times 23 \qquad\qquad\; = 3 \times 2 \times 23$

    The two factorisations are the same (apart from the order in which the factors occur).

2. From the Unique Factorisation Theorem, any two prime factorisations of $a^2 = 2b^2$ are essentially the same. In particular, the two factorisations must have the same number of prime factors.

    This has not happened and so the original assumption, that $\sqrt{2} = \frac{a}{b}$, must be false. $\sqrt{2}$ is therefore irrational.

3. Assume the alternative, that $\sqrt{5} = \frac{a}{b}$

    $$\text{Then } 5b^2 = a^2$$

    If the prime factors of a are $f_1 f_2 f_3 \dots f_n$ say, then

    a^2 has prime factors $(f_1 f_1)(f_2 f_2)$ ... etc.

    Similarly b^2 has prime factors $(p_1 p_1)(p_2 p_2)$ ...

    Then $5b^2$ has an odd number of prime factors whereas a^2 has an even number of prime factors.

    This is a contradiction and so $\sqrt{5}$ cannot be expressed in the form $\frac{a}{b}$. It is therefore irrational.

Fermat's Last Theorem has been proved for $n < 25000$. For $n = 3$, Euler's Conjecture is therefore true since it is the same as the $n = 3$ case of Fermat's 'Theorem'. However, Euler's Conjecture is now totally discredited. A counterexample for $n = 4$ is

$$(2682440)^4 + (15365639)^4 + (18796760)^4 = (20615673)^4$$

The counterexample you were asked to find is for $n = 5$

$$27^5 + 84^5 + 110^5 + 133^5 = 144^5.$$

There are many ways you might have tried to speed up a computer search. Several of these are given below.

(a)   Each of a, b, c and d is at most 143. Rather than letting each variable range from 0 to 143, it is a (small) improvement to consider $a \le b \le c \le d$. Then $0 \le d \le 143$, $0 \le c \le d$, $0 \le b \le c$ and $0 \le a \le b$.

(b)   Fifth powers modulo 25 follow a simple pattern

a	0	1	2	3	4	5	6	7	...
a^5 (mod 25)	0	1	7	18	24	0	1	7	...

Then $a^5 + b^5 + c^5 + d^5 = 144^5$
$\Rightarrow a^5 + b^5 + c^5 + d^5 \equiv 24 \pmod{25}$

The only possibilities for the 5th powers modulo 25 are

$\{0, 0, 0, 24\}$, $\{0, 1, 24, 24\}$ and $\{0, 7, 18, 24\}$.

You can therefore suppose that $a^5 \equiv 0 \pmod{25}$ and $b^5 \equiv 24 \pmod{25}$ i.e.

$a \in \{0, 5, 10, 15 \dots \}$ and $b \in \{4, 9, 14, 19 \dots \}$

(c)   Fifth powers modulo 11 are 0, 1 or 10.

Then $a^5 + b^5 + c^5 + d^5 = 144^5$
$\Rightarrow a^5 + b^5 + c^5 + d^5 \equiv 1 \pmod{11}$

The only possibilities for the 5th powers modulo 11 are $\{0, 0, 0, 1\}$ and $\{0, 1, 1, 10\}$. At least one of a, b, c and d is therefore divisible by 11.

Tutorial sheet

The questions on the tasksheet should provide a good test of whether or not you understand the different types of proof covered in this chapter. Even more importantly, these questions give you the opportunity to have your proofs examined by one or more of your peers to see just how convincing you have been.

For each problem you should discuss what key feature(s) of the conjecture indicate which method of proof is most likely to be successful.

1.   Any whole number is of the form $3a$, $3a + 1$ or $3a + 2$.

$$3a = 3 \times a + 5 \times 0$$
$$3a + 1 = 3(a - 3) + 5 \times 2 \qquad (a \geq 3)$$
$$3a + 2 = 3(a - 1) + 5 \times 1 \qquad (a \geq 2)$$

The conjecture is therefore true.

[It would also be reasonable to prove the result by induction.]

2.   Assume the alternative, that there is a smallest positive number, say x.

Then $\frac{x}{2}$ is a positive number, smaller than x. This contradicts the definition of x. Hence there is no smallest positive number.

3.   A counterexample is $33337 = 37 \times 901$.

4.   It is easy to work out that the numbers are squares of numbers of the form $6 \ldots 67$. A rigorous proof would involve induction but the following argument is likely to convince most people.

$$
\begin{array}{r}
6 \ldots 67 \\
\times\ 6 \\
\hline
40 \ldots 02 \\
\hline
\end{array}
$$

So
$$
\begin{array}{r}
6 \ldots 67 \\
\times\ 6 \ldots 66 \\
\hline
4 \ldots 442 \ldots 22 \\
\hline
\end{array}
$$

Therefore
$$
\begin{array}{r}
6 \ldots 67 \\
\times\ 6 \ldots 67 \\
\hline
4 \ldots\ 442 \ldots 22 \\
6 \ldots 67 \\
\hline
4 \ldots\ 448 \ldots 89 \\
\hline
\end{array}
$$

(continued)

31

5.   You may have realised that an *n*-sided polygon can be split into *n* – 2 triangles.

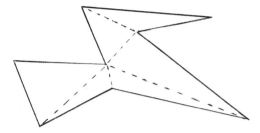

The sum of the internal angles is therefore

$$(n-2) \times \pi = (2n-4) \times \frac{\pi}{2}.$$

However, it is far from easy to give an inductive proof that **any** *n*-sided polygon can be split into *n* – 2 triangles.

6.   Let P(*n*) be the proposition that

$$1 \times n + 2(n-1) + \ldots + n \times 1 = \frac{1}{6}n(n+1)(n+2)$$

$P(1) : 1 \times 1 = \frac{1}{6} \times 1 \times 2 \times 3$ is true.

Assume   P(*k*) is true:
$$1 \times k + 2 \times (k-1) + \ldots + k \times 1 = \frac{1}{6}k(k+1)(k+2)$$

Then $1 \times (k+1) + 2 \times k + \ldots + k \times 2 + (k+1) \times 1$

$= 1 \times k + 1 + 2 \times (k-1) + 2 + \ldots + k \times 1 + k + (k+1)$

$= \frac{1}{6}k(k+1)(k+2) + 1 + 2 + \ldots + (k+1)$

$= \frac{1}{6}k(k+1)(k+2) + \frac{1}{2}(k+1)(k+2)$

$= \frac{1}{6}(k+1)(k+2)(k+3)$

Hence P(*k* + 1) is also true.

By mathematical induction, P(*n*) is true for all natural numbers *n*.

7.   The player's claim is correct but a more precise result is that:

You can always win if the number of matches left for you is **not** a multiple of four. The strategy you must follow is always to leave your opponent a multiple of four matches.

A rigorous proof would require mathematical induction. The crucial point is that whenever your opponent takes *x* matches, $x \in \{1, 2, 3\}$, you then take $4 - x$ matches. In this way, the pile is reduced by four matches after each pair of turns.